This is
My Kit

Written by Paul Harrison
Photographed by Will Amlot

Collins

This is my kit.

lemon

pins

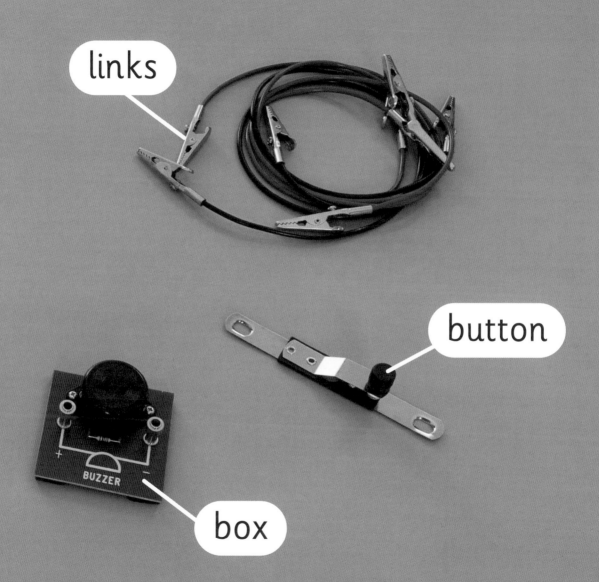

links

button

box

Pick a lemon and cut it.

Push in the metal pins.

long metal pins

Link the pins on.

9

Fix them to the box.

It can go on and off.

/th/

/ng/

14

/ch/

After reading

Letters and Sounds: Phase 3

Word count: 40

Focus phonemes: /th/ /nk/ /x/ /ch/ /ng/ /zz/

Common exception words: my, to, the, go, push

Curriculum links: Understanding the World: Technology

Early learning goals: Listening and attention: children listen attentively in a range of situations; Understanding: answer 'how' and 'why' questions about their experiences and in response to stories or events; Reading: read and understand simple sentences, use phonic knowledge to decode regular words and read them aloud accurately, read some common irregular words, demonstrate understanding when talking with others about what they have read

Developing fluency

- Your child may enjoy hearing you read the book.
- As you read, point out the labels and how they help you to understand the text and the pictures.
- You could take turns to read a page. Model reading with lots of expression and encourage your child to do the same.

Phonic practice

- Look at page 2 together. Point to the word **this** and model sounding it out. Use your finger to draw a line under 'th' as you sound it and to point to 'i' and 's' as you sound them out. Now blend the sounds together. Ask your child to do the same with the words:
  - 'links' on page 3
  - 'chop' on page 5
  - 'them' on page 10.
- Turn to pages 14 and 15 and look for items in the picture that use the phonemes /ng/ /th/ and /ch/ (*think, checklist, chains, thread, thimble, chalk, string, ring, thumbprint, three*).